Helium Resources of the United States—2007

December 2008

Norbert Pacheco
Petroleum Engineer Team Lead
Bureau of Land Management
Amarillo Field Office
Amarillo, Texas

Sherif Fathi Ali
Petroleum Engineer
Bureau of Land Management
Amarillo Field Office
Amarillo, Texas

Technical Note 429

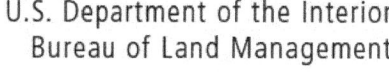

U.S. Department of the Interior
Bureau of Land Management

Unit of Measure Abbreviations
Used in Report

Bcf	billion cubic feet
MMcf	million cubic feet
°F	degree Fahrenheit
%	percent
psia	pounds per square inch, absolute

Suggested Citation:

Pacheco N. and Ali S.F. 2008. Helium Resources of the United States—2007, Technical Note 429. Bureau of Land Management. Denver, Colorado. BLM/NM/ST-09/001+3745. 20 pp.

Contents

Table

Figures

Technical Note 429, Helium Resources of the United States—2007, is an assessment of the total estimated helium reserves and resources of the United States. This assessment is made using estimates of natural gas resources from the Potential Gas Committee (PGC) report, *Potential Supply of Natural Gas in the United States* (December 31, 2006); estimates of proved natural gas reserves from the Department of Energy (DOE), Energy Information Administration (EIA) report, *U.S. Crude Oil, Natural Gas, and Natural Gas Liquids Reserves 2006 Annual Report*; IHS Inc., cumulative gas production data; and data from previous *Helium Resources of the United States* reports. This report is part of the Bureau of Land Management's Amarillo Field Office mission of providing information to the Secretary of the Interior and the public on a limited natural resource that is being depleted.

This report only covers information on helium reserves and resources and does not report on current helium business or other activities that were discussed in previous reports. The report presents a general picture of the current helium resources of the United States and was simplified from previous reports to present a focused view of those resources. Part of the reason for the change was the result of feedback from industry customers that indicated previous reports were hard to analyze. In addition, some of the information that was presented in previous reports is already being reported in the U.S. Geological Survey published *Mineral Commodity Summaries and Mineral Industry Surveys* reports.

The total helium reserves and resources of the United States are estimated to be 732 Bcf as of December 31, 2006. This includes estimated measured reserves from previous helium resources reports, plus calculated reserves from DOE/EIA estimates of proved natural gas reserves and IHS Inc., cumulative gas production data, and estimated probable, possible, and speculative helium resources calculated from PGC estimates of natural gas resources for the seven PGC regions. The total resources include approximately 24 Bcf of helium being stored at the Federal Government's Cliffside Gasfield Reserve in Potter County, Texas.

Technical Note 429, Helium Resources of the United States—2007, is an assessment of the total estimated helium reserves and resources of the United States. This assessment is made using estimates of natural gas resources from the Potential Gas Committee (PGC) report, *Potential Supply of Natural Gas in the United States* (December 31, 2006) (1); estimates of proved natural gas reserves from the Department of Energy (DOE), Energy Information Administration (EIA) report, *U.S. Crude Oil, Natural Gas, and Natural Gas Liquids Reserves 2006 Annual Report* (2); IHS Inc., cumulative gas production data; and data from previous *Helium Resources of the United States reports*.

The total helium reserves and resources of the United States are estimated to be 732 Bcf[1] as of December 31, 2006. These include 151 Bcf of **measured** helium reserves (including approximately 24 Bcf stored at Cliffside Field), 189 Bcf of **probable** helium resources, 210 Bcf of **possible** helium resources, and 182 Bcf of **speculative** helium resources[2].

The average helium contents for each of the seven Potential Gas Committee (PGC) regions (Figure 1) were used to calculate the estimated measured reserves. The probable, possible, and speculative helium resources were estimated using the PGC estimates of natural gas resources for the seven PGC regions and the average helium contents as well (Table 1). The average helium contents used in this report are those used in the previous helium resources report, *Helium Resources of the United States–2003 (Technical Note 415)*.

Most of the estimated measured helium reserves (151 Bcf) are contained in gas fields from which helium is currently being extracted. Current helium extraction in the United States occurs mostly from natural gases produced from the Hugoton gas area (Mid-Continent Area) in Kansas, Oklahoma, and Texas, and the Riley Ridge area (Rocky Mountain Area) in southwestern Wyoming (Figure 2). Helium extracted from natural gas in the United States in 2006 was approximately 2.9 Bcf, while helium withdrawn from the Cliffside Field Reserve was about 2.1 Bcf.

This publication is the 14th in a series of reports on the helium resources of the United States. The first of these reports gave information on helium resources as of January 1, 1973. These reports have been published approximately every 2 years with the last report, *Helium Resources of the United States–2003 (Technical Note 415)*, providing information as of December 31, 2002 (3).

The Helium Operations Office in Amarillo, Texas, has been estimating the helium resources of the Nation for almost 60 years in connection with a search for helium occurrences that has been conducted for over 80 years. These activities are carried on:

---

[1]All values in this report, unless otherwise stated, ate at 14.65 psia and 60 °F as of December 31, 2006.
[2]See Glossary for definitions of resource terms.

(1) to ensure a continuing supply of helium to meet essential Federal and commercial needs, (2) to provide information to the Secretary of the Interior so that helium resources reserved to the United States on Federal land can be properly managed, and (3) to provide the public with information on a limited natural resource that is being depleted.

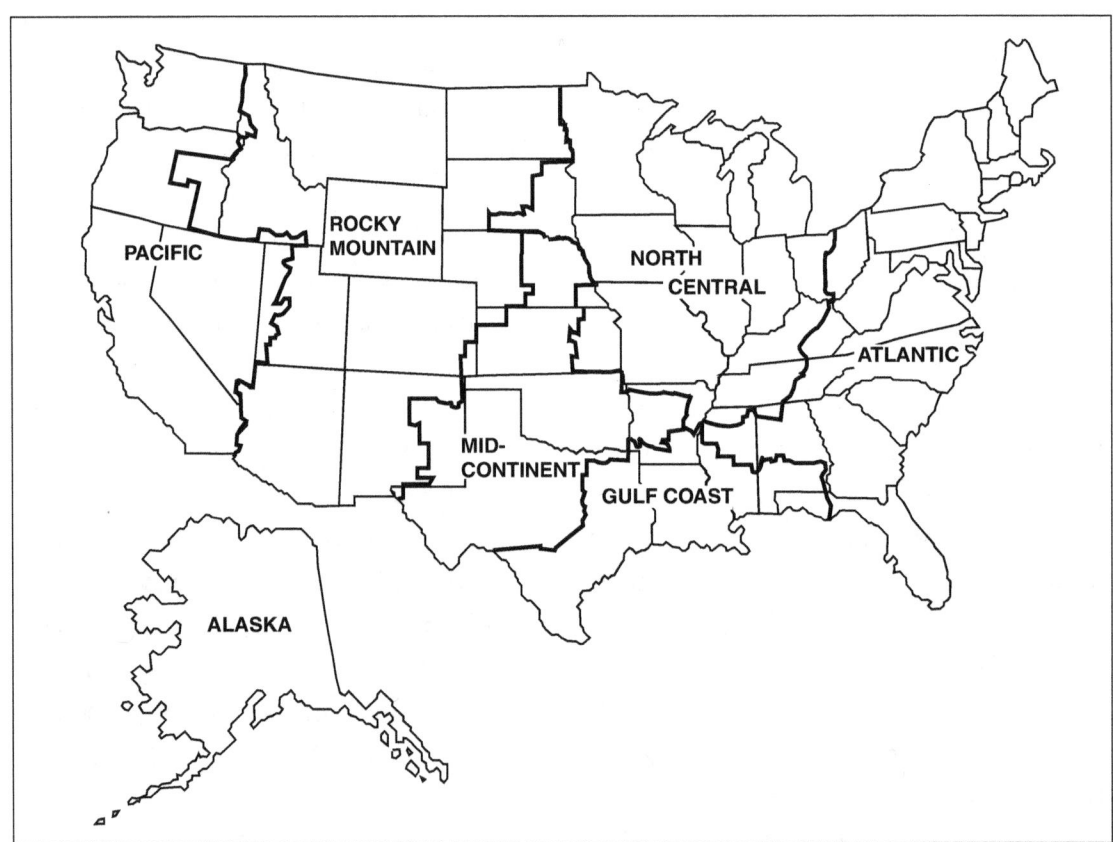

Figure 1. Map of potential Gas Committee (PGC) Regions.

Table 1. Estimated Helium Reserves and Resources by Potential Gas Committee Regions as of December 31, 2006
(all volumes in billion cubic feet at 14.65 PSIA and 60° F).

Region	Measured Helium Reserves	Probable Helium Resources	Possible Helium Resources	Speculative Helium Resources	Total Helium
Alaska	1.14[1]	3.44	1.83	3.09	9.50
Atlantic	5.20[2]	12.89	12.97	1.58	32.64
Gulf Coast	0.78[3]	4.52	5.11	5.61	16.02
Mid-Continent	65.67[4]	85.48	100.58	89.76	341.49
North-Central	1.14[5]	0.68	1.45	3.78	7.05
Pacific	0.38[6]	0.23	1.68	1.60	3.89
Rocky Mountain	76.47[7]	82.00	86.88	76.09	321.44
Total USA	150.78[8]	189.24[9]	210.50[10]	181.51[11]	732.03[12]

1, 2, 3, 5, 6, 7	Calculated from proved (Dry Natural Gas) reserves from DOE/EIA December 31, 2006 report on U. S. Crude Oil, Natural Gas, and Natural Gas Liquids Reserves
4	Includes 2.3 Bcf of helium contained in Cliffside Field native gas and 23.84 Bcf of helium in Cliffside Field storage. Calculated from IHS Inc., cumulative gas production data; Cliffside Field native helium and stored helium from December 2006 BLM Statistical Report
8, 12	Includes 2.3 Bcf of helium contained in Cliffside Field native gas and 23.84 Bcf of helium in Cliffside Field storage
9, 10, 11	Calculated from estimates of natural gas resources from the Potential Gas Committee (PGC) report, Potential Supply of Natural Gas in the United States (December 31, 2006)

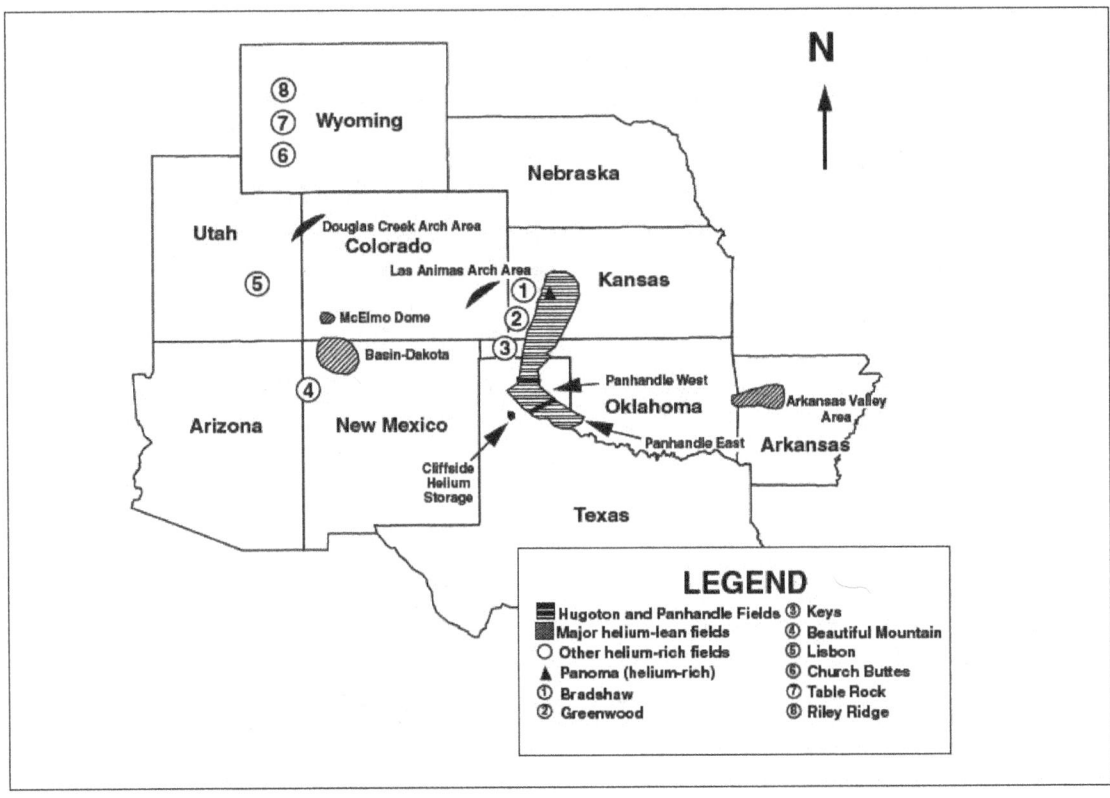

Figure 2. Location of Major Helium-Bearing Gasfields.

Measured Helium Reserves

The total measured helium reserves of the United States are estimated to be about 151 Bcf. This includes the Federal Government's and private companies' helium stored at Cliffside Field. In past reports, these reserves were subdivided and reported as measured, measured marginal, and measured subeconomic. This report only presents the total estimated measured helium reserves for each PGC region. Some of the reserves were estimated using data from previous helium resources reports and some were calculated using DOE/EIA estimates of proved natural gas reserves and IHS Inc., cumulative gas production data to which known helium contents were applied. The majority of the measured helium reserves are located in the Mid-Continent and Rocky Mountain regions of the United States where most of the helium extraction occurs. Most domestic extracted helium comes from the Hugoton field in Kansas, Oklahoma, and Texas; the Panoma field in Kansas; the Keyes field in Oklahoma; the Panhandle West and Cliffside fields in Texas; and the Riley Ridge area in Wyoming (Figure 2).

All measured (proved) reserve estimates involve some degree of uncertainty, depending mainly on the amount and reliability of the geologic and engineering data available at the time of the estimate and the interpretation of those data. The relative degree of uncertainty may be conveyed by classifying reserves as either proved or unproved. The proved (measured) reserves are the estimated quantities which the geological and engineering data demonstrate with reasonable certainty to be recoverable in future years from known reservoirs under existing economic and operating conditions. However, since petroleum engineering and geological judgments are required in estimating proved reserves, the results are not precise measurements. Unproved reserves are less certain to be recovered and may be classified as probable or possible to indicate progressively increasing uncertainty.

Potential Helium Resources

The PGC reports estimates of natural gas resources for seven regions of the United States (Figure 1). These estimated natural gas resources are used to evaluate the potential helium resources of the United States. The total potential helium resources of the United States are estimated to be about 581 Bcf. These include 189 Bcf of probable helium resources, 210 Bcf of possible helium resources, and 182 Bcf of speculative (most likely) helium resources. The estimated potential helium resources of 581 Bcf, as of December 31, 2006, are 212 Bcf more than the estimated 369 Bcf potential helium resources based on PGC estimates of natural gas resources as of December 31, 2002. This large increase in potential helium resources between 2002 and 2006 results from the substantial increased estimates of natural gas resources reported by the PGC in their 2006 report. The potential helium resources, based on the PGC's estimates of natural gas resources at yearend in 2002 and 2006, are as follows:

Category	2002	2006
Probable Helium (Bcf)	117	189
Possible Helium (Bcf)	149	210
Speculative Helium (Bcf)	103	182
Total	**369**	**581**

The helium contents used in estimating the helium reserves and resources for this report are the average helium contents used in the last helium resources report, *Helium Resources of the United States–2003 (Technical Note 415)*. Helium reserves were estimated using DOE/EIA proved gas reserves data for December 31, 2006, and IHS Inc., cumulative gas production data. The helium reserves calculated using IHS Inc., production data are based on natural gas cumulative production history data with respect to pressure and compressibility factor (z) changes over time. In both cases, the average helium content for each PGC region was applied to the gas reserves and/or production data. The probable, possible, and speculative helium resources were estimated in the same manner, but from the PGC's December 31, 2006, estimates of natural gas resources. The average helium contents for the seven PGC Regions are shown below.

PGC Region	Avg. Helium Content (%)
Alaska	0.0111
Atlantic	0.0285
Gulf Coast	0.0053
Mid-Continent	0.1421
North Central	0.0371
Pacific	0.0069
Rocky Mountain	0.1173

In previous Bureau reports, it was concluded that relatively large volumes of helium would be available from natural gas through 2020. It was assumed that most of the helium would be extracted from gases with leaner concentrations than those being processed today. However, increased demand for helium in recent years, particularly increased exports of U.S. produced helium, has resulted in the Federal Government's Cliffside Field Reserve playing a vital role in helping to supply the increased worldwide helium demand. It was anticipated that the new helium extraction facilities in Qatar and the Skikda plant in Algeria would add significant helium production to the world market by 2006. However, due to operational problems, helium extraction from these two plants has been much less than anticipated. It is expected that once these two plants start producing helium at plant capacity rates, and/or additional new sources of helium come online, helium demand on Cliffside Field will decline over time. However, it is probable that production from Cliffside Field will continue to supply the helium needed to help meet worldwide helium demand indefinitely.

According to advances in natural gas extraction and liquification technology, helium extraction and processing is no longer a cost intensive process; in other words, it is not necessary that helium occur in concentrations of 0.3% or more to be economical for production. Helium could occur in very low concentrations and still be processed as an economical product for marketing and sales. Also, the high market price of natural gas and natural gas byproducts, such as nitrogen and helium, is a good incentive for exploration of new gasfields and the production of helium among other gases. The high market prices are a driving force for increased exploration and re-evaluating reserve estimates.

As of December 31, 2006, there were 23.8 Bcf of helium stored in Bush Dome at Cliffside Field. About 22.5 Bcf of the stored helium is owned by the Federal Government and 1.3 Bcf is owned by private companies. There are also approximately 2.3 Bcf of helium contained in the native gas in Bush Dome. The Helium Privatization Act of 1996 requires that Federal Government owned helium in excess of 600 MMcf be offered for sale by January 1, 2015. At the current rate of depletion, the Federal Government Reserve at Cliffside Field is expected to be depleted by 2020.

References

1. Potential Gas Committee. 2007. Potential Supply of Natural Gas in the United States (as of December 31, 2006). Potential Gas Agency, Colorado School of Mines. Golden, Colorado. 424 pp.

2. Department of Energy, Energy Information Administration. 2007. U.S. Crude Oil, Natural Gas, and Natural Gas Liquids Reserves 2006 Annual Report. DOE/EIA 0216 (2007). 17 pp.

3. Gage, B.D., and D.L. Driskill. 2004. Helium Resources of the United States—2003, Technical Note 415. Bureau of Land Management. Denver, Colorado. BLM/NM/ST-04/002+3745. 35 pp.

Bibliography

Driskill, D.L. 2008. Analyses of Natural Gases, 2005–2007, Technical Note 427. Bureau of Land Management. Denver, Colorado. BLM/NM/ST-08/007+3700. 199 pp.

Gage, B.D., and D.L. Driskill. 1998. Helium Resources of the United States—1997, Technical Note 403. Bureau of Land Management. Denver, Colorado. BLM/NM/ST-02/001+3700. 28 pp.

Gage, B.D., and D.L. Driskill. 2001. Helium Resources of the United States—2001, Technical Note 408. Bureau of Land Management. Denver, Colorado. BLM/NM/ST-2/001+3700. 30 pp.

Gage, B.D., and D.L. Driskill. 1998. Analyses of Natural Gases, 1996-97, Technical Note 404. Bureau of Land Management. Denver, Colorado. BLM/HE/ST-98/0033700. 71 pp.

Gage, B.D., and D.L. Driskill. 2003. Analyses of Natural Gases, 1998-2001, Technical Note 412. Bureau of Land Management. Denver, Colorado. BLM/NM/ST-03/001+3700. 173 pp.

Gage, B.D., and D.L. Driskill. 2005. Analyses of Natural Gases, 2002-2004, Technical Note 418. Bureau of Land Management. Denver, Colorado. BLM/NM/ST-06/003+3700. 243 pp.

Hamak, J.E., and D.L. Driskill. 1995. Helium Resources of the United States—1993. BuMines IC 9436. 18 pp.

U. S. Department of the Interior, U.S. Geological Survey. 2008. Mineral Commodity Summaries at *http://minerals.usgs.gov/minerals/pubs/mcs/* (page last modified: Monday, 11-Feb-2008).

U. S. Department of the Interior, U.S. Geological Survey. 2008. Mineral Industry Surveys at *http://minerals.usgs.gov/minerals/pubs/commodity/mis.html* (page last modified: Tuesday, 19-Aug-2008).

Glossary of Reserve and Resource Terms

The following definitions were developed from definitions found in the DOE/EIA publication, *U.S. Crude Oil, Natural Gas, and Natural Gas Liquids Reserves 2006 Annual Report* (November 2007), and from PGC definitions in previous helium resources reports.

Measured Reserves – The estimated reserves, which geological and engineering data demonstrate with reasonable certainty to be recoverable in future years from known reservoirs under existing economic and operating conditions. Petroleum engineering and geological judgment are required in estimating proved (measured) reserves; therefore, the results are not precise measurements.

Probable Resources – Those resources associated with known gasfields which are most likely to be produced. Substantial geologic and engineering data are available on this type resource. Probable resources bridge the boundary between discovered and undiscovered resources. The discovered portion includes supply from future extensions of existing pools in known productive reservoirs. The pools containing these resources have been discovered, but the extent of the pools has not been completely delineated by development drilling. Therefore, the existence and quantity of resources in the undrilled portion of the pools is unconfirmed. The undiscovered portion is expected to come from future new pool discoveries within existing fields either in productive reservoirs in those fields or in other formations known to be productive elsewhere in the same geologic province or subprovince.

Possible Resources – Those resources that are less assured because they are postulated to exist outside of known gasfields, but are associated with a productive formation in a productive province. Their occurrence is indicated by a projection of plays or trends of a producing formation into a less well-explored area of the same geologic province or subprovince. The resources are expected to be found in new field discoveries, postulated to occur within these trends or plays under both similar or different geologic conditions.

Speculative Resources – Those resources that are expected to be found in formations or provinces that have not yet proven to be productive. Geologic analogs are developed in order to ensure reasonable evaluations of these unknown resources. The resources are anticipated from new pools or new field discoveries in formations not previously productive within a productive geologic province and/or from new field discoveries within a geologic province not previously productive.

Appendix A

Estimated average helium contents of gas resources by PGC regions and basins

Region and Basin		Avg. Helium Content	Footnotes
Alaska		**0.0111%**	1
Atlantic:			
P-100	New England and Adirondack Uplifts	0.0233%	1
P-110	Atlantic Coastal Basin	0.0233%	1
P-120	Appalachian Basin	0.0497%	1
P-130	Piedmont-Blue Ridge Province	0.0497%	1
P-140	South Georgia-Peninsular Florida	0.0150%	1
P-150	Black Warrior Basin	0.0100%	1
	Average	**0.0285%**	
Gulf Coast:			
P-300	Louisiana-Mississippi-Alabama Salt Dome	0.0430%	1
P-310	Louisiana Gulf Coast Basin	0.0020%	1
P-320	East Texas Basin	0.0017%	1
P-330	Texas Gulf Coast Basin	0.0020%	1
P-930	Eastern Gulf Shelf	0.0014%	2
P-931	Eastern Gulf Slope	0.0014%	1
P-935	Louisiana Shelf	0.0014%	2
P-936	Louisiana Slope	0.0014%	2
P-940	Texas Shelf	0.0014%	2
P-941	Texas Slope	0.0014%	2
P-945	Gulf of Mexico Outer Continental Slope	0.0014%	1
	Average	**0.0053%**	
Mid-continent:			
P-400	Central Kansas Uplift, Salina Basin	0.2081%	1
P-410	Arkoma Basin	0.0110%	1
P-420	Anadarko, Palo Duro Basins, etc	0.2081%	1
P-430	Fort Worth and Strawn Basins, Bend Arch	0.2550%	1
P-440	Permian Basin	0.0282%	1
	Average	**0.1421%**	
North Central		**0.0371%**	1
Pacific		**0.0069%**	1

Estimated average helium contents of gas resources by PGC regions and basins

Region and Basin		Avg. Helium Content	Footnotes
Rocky Mountain:			
P-500	Williston Basin	0.0802%	1
P-510	Powder River Basin	0.0793%	1
P-515	Big Horn Basin	0.0490%	1
P-520	Wind River Basin	0.0417%	1
P-530	Greater Green River Basin < 15,000 ft.	0.0760%	1
P-530	Greater Green River Basin > 15,000 ft.	0.5190%	3
P-535	Denver Basin, Chadron Arch and Las Animas Arch	0.0642%	1
P-540	Uinta/Piceance Basins; Park and Eagle Basins	0.1720%	1
P-545	San Juan Mountains; San Louis and Raton Basins	0.0230%	2
P-550	Paradox Basin	0.4150%	1
P-555	San Juan Basin	0.0228%	1
P-560	Southern Basin and Range Province	0.0150%	2
P-565	Plateau Province, Black Mesa Basin	0.0070%	2
P-570	Sweetgrass Arch	0.1602%	1
P-575	Montana Folded Belt	0.1602%	1
P-580	Snake River Basin	0.0275%	1
P-590	Wyoming-Utah-Idaho Thrust Belt	0.0824%	1
	Average	**0.1173%**	

FOOTNOTES:

1. The average helium content is weighted based on the number of gas samples from each formation and field combination in the region.

2. The average helium content is derived from pipeline gas surveys carried out by the Bureau and are weighted based on gas volumes flowing through gas plants in the region.

3. The average helium content is weighted heavily to the high helium-bearing gas in the Riley Ridge field. The helium contents of other gases in the area also are considered.